I0843637

*"And he who saves a life shall be as if he
had given life to all mankind."
(Holy Quran 5:32)*

In today's interconnected world, the lines between information technology (IT) and operational technology (OT) continue to blur, leading to the convergence of two distinct domains. The interconnection and data exchange between SCADA (Supervisory Control and Data Acquisition) systems, which are a crucial subset of OT, and conventional IT systems has given rise to unique challenges, especially in the realm of security and audit. "Auditing SCADA and OT Systems: A Guide for IT Auditors" was conceived to bridge this gap, providing IT auditors with a comprehensive understanding of SCADA and OT systems, and equipping them with the knowledge and tools necessary to audit these systems effectively.

While many books explore the technical nuances of SCADA and OT, few delve deep into the intricacies of auditing such systems from an IT auditor's perspective. As industries and critical infrastructures increasingly rely on SCADA and OT for their operations, the need for robust and tailored auditing approaches has never been more crucial. This book, therefore, serves as both an introduction to the world of SCADA and OT and a guide for IT auditors, offering insights, methodologies, and practical advice for those tasked with ensuring the security and resilience of these critical systems.

Before diving into the content, I'd like to take a moment to express my deepest gratitude to those who have supported me throughout this journey. To my family , and the wonderful kids at our home - your unwavering love and encouragement have been my bedrock. To my teachers, friends and colleagues, your insights and camaraderie have been invaluable.

Remembering with gratitude late Mr. KunniKoya, whose boundless to build my technology skills has left an indelible mark on my life. His belief in my potential and his guidance have shaped my journey, and his legacy continues to inspire me.I am also immensely grateful to my mentors and inspirations Mr. Abdulla AlJawi, Ms. Shaikha AlJerman, Mr. Ali Kashwani, Mr. Sayed Ahmed AlMoosawi, Mr. Ilyas Kooliyangal, Eng Jowher Areecode, Mr. Anwer Naha and Dr. Paul Irving, whose expertise and mentorship have been instrumental and have been invaluable. Your collective wisdom has helped me complete this book.

In the pages that follow, we will embark on a journey of exploration, understanding, and mastery. Whether you're an experienced IT auditor or new to the field, this book aims to provide you with the insights and tools you need to navigate the world of SCADA and OT systems effectively. Let's begin.

How to Use This Book

" Auditing SCADA and OT Systems: A Guide for IT Auditors " is designed to be both a comprehensive introduction to the world of SCADA and OT systems and a practical guide for IT auditors. Whether you are a seasoned auditor venturing into the OT space or a newcomer to the world of IT auditing, this book has been structured to provide you with a clear pathway for understanding and assessing SCADA and OT systems. Here's how to make the most of it:

1. Start at the Beginning : While seasoned professionals might be tempted to skip introductory sections, it's advisable to start from Chapter 1. The foundational knowledge laid out in the initial chapters sets the stage for the deeper dives in later sections.

2. Engage with Case Studies : Throughout the book, real-world case studies highlight the challenges and solutions associated with SCADA and OT systems auditing. These are not just cautionary tales but learning opportunities. Reflect on them, discuss them with peers, and consider the implications they might have on your work.

3. Utilize the Appendices : The appendices contain a wealth of supplementary material, including glossaries, checklists, and further readings. These resources can be invaluable during actual audits, so familiarize yourself with them and keep them handy.

4. Participate in Group Discussions : If you're reading this as part of a team or study group, engage in group discussions. Debating and discussing the content can provide new perspectives and a deeper understanding.

5. Practice with the Templates : Auditing is as much a practical skill as it is a theoretical one. The book includes various templates and checklists designed for real-world application. Use these in your audits, adapt them as necessary, and reflect on your experiences to refine your approach.

6. Stay Updated : The world of SCADA and OT systems is dynamic. While this book provides a comprehensive overview and guide, always stay updated with the latest developments in the field. We recommend setting up alerts or joining relevant professional groups to stay informed.

7. Seek Feedback : As you apply the knowledge and techniques from this book in your auditing practice, seek feedback from colleagues, superiors, and even clients.

Continuous feedback is key to growth and mastery.

8. Revisit Often : This book is not meant to be read once and then shelved. As you grow in your career and face new challenges in the field of SCADA and OT systems auditing, revisit relevant sections. The insights and methodologies outlined here will remain relevant and can provide guidance in various situations.

In essence, this book is more than just a reading material; it's a tool. Approach it with an open mind, engage with its content actively, and apply its teachings in your professional journey. The world of SCADA and OT systems auditing is vast and ever-evolving, and this guide aims to be your trusted companion along the way.

Contents

Introduction......................1

How to Use This Book....4

Chapter 1: Introduction to SCADA and OT Systems 10

Chapter 2: Key Components of SCADA and OT Systems............22

Chapter 3: Threat Landscape for SCADA and OT System..............29

Chapter 4: Fundamentals of Auditing SCADA and OT Systems....................36

Chapter 5: Risk Assessment and Management for SCADA/OT 44

Chapter 6: Auditing SCADA and OT Network Infrastructure 53

Chapter 7: Auditing Physical Security and Environment 64

Chapter 8: Auditing Human Factors and Training 72

Chapter 9: Auditing Backup and Recovery Procedures 81

Chapter10: Compliance and Regulatory Considerations 89

Chapter11: Reporting and Follow-Up of Audit Findings on SCADA and OT Systems...................98

Appendix 106

Glossary of terms 107

References and Further Readings.......................110

Chapter 1: Introduction to SCADA and OT Systems

Welcome to the fascinating world of SCADA and OT systems! If you've ever wondered how factories automate their processes, how power grids are managed, or how water treatment plants ensure we have clean water, then you're in for a treat. This chapter will introduce you to the fundamental concepts of SCADA and OT systems, their historical evolution, their significance in modern industries, and the key distinctions between IT and OT environments. Let's dive in!

1.1 What are OT, ICS and SCADA Systems?

SCADA (Supervisory Control and Data Acquisition), ICS (Industrial Control Systems), and OT (Operational Technology) are terms related to the automation and control of industrial processes. Here's a detailed definition of each term along with their differences:

SCADA (Supervisory Control and Data Acquisition)

SCADA is a system of software and hardware elements that allows industrial organizations to control industrial processes locally or at remote locations, monitor, gather, and process real-time data, and directly interact with devices such as sensors, valves, pumps, motors, and more through human-machine interface (HMI) software.

Components i consists of field data interface devices (sensors and actuators), communication networks, data processing units, and user interfaces (HMIs).

SCADA is used in various industries including water and wastewater, energy, oil and gas, and manufacturing.

Compared to ICS and OT, SCADA systems tend to focus more on the data acquisition and remote monitoring aspects of industrial control, often providing a higher level of data visualization and analysis tools.

ICS (Industrial Control Systems)

ICS is a general term that encompasses different types of control systems used in industrial production, including SCADA systems, distributed control systems (DCS), and other smaller control system configurations such as programmable logic controllers (PLC).

ICS components Includes the control systems themselves (like SCADA, DCS, PLC), networked systems, and various field devices.

ICS systems are broadly used across industries such as manufacturing, energy, water treatment, and transportation.

ICS is a broader term that includes SCADA as a subset. While SCADA focuses on data acquisition and monitoring, ICS encompasses the entire spectrum of industrial control, from data acquisition to process control.

OT (Operational Technology)

OT refers to the hardware and software used to monitor and control physical processes, devices, and infrastructure.

Components of OT Includes industrial control systems like SCADA and DCS, sensors, actuators, and industrial networks.

OT systems are sued in critical infrastructure and industries like energy, manufacturing, and transportation.

OT is a broader category that includes both ICS and SCADA. While ICS and SCADA are focused on industrial control and automation, OT encompasses all technologies that interact with the physical world, even extending beyond industrial settings.

Key Differences:

Scope: OT has the broadest scope, including all technology that interacts with the physical world. ICS is a subset of OT, focusing specifically on industrial control. SCADA is a subset of ICS, with a specific focus on data acquisition and remote monitoring.

Functionality : SCADA is tailored for remote monitoring and data acquisition, ICS encompasses a broader range of control functionalities, and OT includes all technologies dealing with the monitoring and control of physical processes.

Applications: While all three are used in industrial settings, OT's applications can extend beyond industry, covering infrastructure and other areas where physical processes need to be monitored and controlled.

In summary, while there are overlaps between SCADA, ICS, and OT, they represent different scopes and aspects of industrial control and automation, with SCADA focusing on data acquisition and remote monitoring, ICS covering a broader range of industrial control systems, and OT encompassing all technologies interacting with the physical world.

1.2 Historical Development of SCADA and OT

The roots of SCADA and OT can be traced back to the 1960s when industries began to automate their processes using mainframe computers. These early systems were rudimentary, relying on wired connections and analog signals.

The 1980s saw the advent of microprocessors, leading to more sophisticated and decentralized SCADA systems. These systems could now communicate using digital signals, improving efficiency and reliability.

The turn of the century brought about the integration of SCADA with the internet, paving the way for modern SCADA systems that can be accessed and controlled remotely, offering unprecedented flexibility and scalability.

Today, with the rise of Industry 4.0 and the Internet of Things (IoT), OT systems are smarter, interconnected, and integral to the functioning of modern industries.

1.3 Importance of SCADA and OT in Modern Industries

In today's fast-paced industrial landscape, SCADA and OT systems are indispensable. Here's why:

Efficiency : Automation reduces manual intervention, leading to faster and more consistent processes.

Monitoring: Real-time data acquisition allows industries to detect anomalies instantly, preventing potential disasters.

Optimization: By analyzing the vast amounts of data collected, industries can optimize their operations, leading to cost savings and increased productivity.

Remote Control: Industries are no longer bound by geography. A SCADA system can control wind farms in Europe from a control center in Asia!

From oil and gas to food production, SCADA and OT have revolutionized the way industries operate, driving growth and innovation.

1.4 Differences between IT and OT Environments

Immediately, IT (Information Technology) and OT might seem similar, but they cater to different needs and have distinct characteristics:

Purpose: IT systems focus on data processing and storage, ensuring the flow of information. OT systems, however, control physical processes and devices.

Integrity vs. Confidentiality: In IT, data confidentiality is paramount. In OT, the integrity and availability of the system take precedence to ensure continuous operations.

Interactivity: IT environments are interactive, with regular data exchanges. OT environments, in contrast, are often isolated, prioritizing stability and reliability.

Updates & Patches : IT systems frequently undergo software updates. OT systems, due to their critical nature, might not be updated as often to avoid disruptions.

Understanding these distinctions is crucial for anyone venturing into SCADA and OT systems, especially when considering security and auditing practices.

We hope this introduction has provided you with a clear understanding of SCADA and OT systems. As we move forward, we'll delve deeper into the intricacies of these systems and their significance in today's industrial landscape. Stay curious and keep reading!

Chapter 2: Key Components of SCADA and OT Systems

Ah, the heart of the matter! As we delve into the world of SCADA and OT systems, understanding their key components is crucial. Think of these systems as intricate puzzles; each piece, whether hardware or software, plays a pivotal role in creating a cohesive whole. This chapter will guide you through these pieces, giving you a clear picture of how they fit together. Let's embark on this journey!

2.1 Hardware Components

Behind every great software, there's a piece of hardware running it. And in SCADA and OT systems, this hardware isn't just your ordinary computer or server. Let's explore!

PLCs (Programmable Logic Controllers)

PLCs are like the brains behind the operation. These industrial digital computers have been tailored for specific tasks such as controlling machinery on factory assembly lines. For example, in a soda bottling plant, a PLC might ensure that each bottle is filled precisely before moving to the capping stage.

RTUs (Remote Terminal Units)

Think of RTUs as the distant cousins of PLCs. While PLCs might be on-site, RTUs are designed to be placed in remote areas, collecting data and sending it back to a central system. An RTU monitoring a remote pipeline's pressure is a classic example.

IEDs (Intelligent Electronic Devices)

IEDs are smart devices that make decisions based on the data they receive. For instance, in an electric grid, an IED might automatically reroute power if it detects a fault in a line.

Communication Equipment

This is the messenger of the SCADA world. These devices, which include modems, routers, and switches, ensure that data flows seamlessly from one component to another.

2.2 Software Components

Now that we've looked at the hardware, let's dive into the software that brings these systems to life.

HMI (Human-Machine Interface)

HMI is where humans and machines meet. It provides a visual representation of the SCADA system, allowing operators to see data in real-time and control the system. Imagine a touchscreen displaying a water treatment plant's various tanks and valves, letting operators adjust settings with just a tap.

Data Historians

As the name suggests, these are the historians of the SCADA world. They collect and store data over time, allowing for trend analysis and performance reviews. For example, a factory might use a data historian to track its machinery's efficiency over months or years.

SCADA Master Stations

The overseers of the system, SCADA master stations, collect data from all components and make centralized decisions. In a traffic management system, the master station might adjust traffic light timings based on data from various intersections.

2.3 Network Infrastructure

With the hardware and software in place, how do these components talk to each other? Let's delve into the world of networks!

Network Topologies

Just as roads can have different layouts—grids, circles, or dead-ends—networks too have various structures. Common topologies include star, where devices connect to a central point, and ring, where each device connects to two others forming a loop.

Communication Protocols

Protocols are the languages of the SCADA world. They define how data is transmitted and received. Modbus and DNP3 are two widely used SCADA communication protocols.

Remote Access Methods

Sometimes, operators need to access SCADA systems from afar. Remote access methods, such as VPNs (Virtual Private Networks), allow them to securely log in and control the system, even from the other side of the world.

As we wrap up this chapter, remember: SCADA and OT systems are like intricate symphonies, with each component playing its unique note. Understanding these components is the first step in mastering the beautiful, complex world of SCADA and OT. Stay curious and keep exploring!

Chapter 3: Threat Landscape for SCADA

and OT System

In the vast realm of technology, SCADA and OT systems stand as the silent sentinels, orchestrating and overseeing critical operations that our modern society depends upon. Yet, like any technological marvel, these systems are not impervious to threats. Understanding the vulnerabilities and the potential impacts of breaches is paramount. In this chapter, we will navigate the intricate threat landscape, drawing from real-world case studies to illuminate the inherent risks and the devastating consequences of compromise.

3.1 Common Threats and Vulnerabilities

Every system, no matter how robust, has its weak points, and SCADA/OT systems are no exception. Let's delve into some of the most common threats and vulnerabilities that these systems face.

External Threats : These originate from outside the organization. Hackers, whether motivated by profit, political reasons, or mere curiosity, can exploit vulnerabilities to gain unauthorized access. Common methods include phishing attacks, malware, and exploiting unpatched software.

Insider Threats : Surprisingly, one of the most significant risks comes from within the organization. Disgruntled employees, contractors, or even uninformed staff can inadvertently cause breaches or intentionally sabotage systems.

Physical Threats : This includes everything from natural disasters, such as floods or fires, to intentional acts like theft or vandalism that can disrupt system hardware.

System and Software Vulnerabilities: Outdated software, unpatched systems, and misconfigured equipment can leave gaping holes for attackers to exploit. A company neglecting to update its OT software might be vulnerable to a known exploit. An attacker can leverage this vulnerability to infiltrate the system and manipulate its operations.

3.2 Case Studies: Historical Attacks on SCADA/OT Systems

History, often, is our best teacher. Let's turn the pages back and examine some infamous attacks on SCADA/OT systems to understand their origins, execution, and implications.

Stuxnet (2010) : Perhaps the most famous example, Stuxnet was a malicious computer worm that targeted Iranian nuclear facilities. It exploited multiple zero-day vulnerabilities and caused substantial damage by making centrifuges spin out of control, all while displaying normal readings to operators.

Ukraine Power Grid Attack (2015) : In a chilling display of cyber warfare, attackers successfully blacked out a portion of Ukraine's power grid, leaving over 200,000 residents without electricity in the heart of winter.

Triton (2017) : This malware targeted industrial safety systems, aiming to cause physical damage to the equipment. If not detected in time, the consequences could have been catastrophic.

3.3 Potential Impacts of a Compromised SCADA/OT System

When SCADA or OT systems are compromised, the consequences can be far-reaching.

Operational Disruption: The most immediate impact is the halt or disruption of operations. This can result in financial losses and operational setbacks.

Physical Harm: Systems controlling critical infrastructure, like water treatment or power generation, can cause real-world harm if manipulated maliciously.

Economic Consequences: A halt in operations can result in significant financial losses. Additionally, post-breach recovery and litigation can further strain resources.

Reputational Damage: A breach can erode trust among stakeholders, partners, and customers, leading to long-term reputational harm.

Imagine a water treatment facility where the SCADA system is compromised. The attacker alters the chemical mixture, making the water unsafe. This not only disrupts the facility's operations but could also lead to health crises for consumers.

In conclusion, the threat landscape for SCADA and OT systems is vast and varied. But by understanding these threats, learning from historical breaches, and comprehending the potential impacts, we can better prepare and defend against them. As the saying goes, forewarned is forearmed.

Chapter 4: Fundamentals of Auditing SCADA and OT Systems

In the rapidly evolving landscape of SCADA (Supervisory Control and Data Acquisition) and OT (Operational Technology) systems, the need for effective and rigorous auditing practices cannot be overstated. As IT auditors, understanding the nuances of these systems, the standards that guide their operation, and the methodology for their evaluation is paramount. This chapter delves deep into the fundamentals, offering clarity, insights, and actionable guidance for those embarking on the journey of SCADA and OT systems auditing.

4.1 Purpose and Objectives of SCADA/OT Systems Auditing

Why do we audit SCADA and OT systems? This question is fundamental.

Purpose:

The primary purpose of auditing SCADA and OT systems is to assess the security, reliability, and performance of these systems, ensuring that they operate effectively and efficiently, without compromising the integrity and availability of critical infrastructure and processes they control.

Objectives:

- Risk Identification : Uncover vulnerabilities and threats that could compromise the system, potentially leading to financial losses, operational disruptions, or safety hazards.

- Regulatory Compliance : Ensure that SCADA and OT systems comply with relevant industry regulations, standards, and best practices.

- Operational Efficiency : Evaluate the performance and efficiency of the system, identifying areas for potential improvement or optimization.

- Data Integrity : Ensure that data generated and processed by SCADA and OT systems is accurate, reliable, and free from unauthorized tampering.

Case Study: The Maroochy Water Breach
In 2000, a disgruntled employee exploited vulnerabilities in the Maroochy Shire's wastewater management system in Australia. Over a span of two months, he released millions of liters of raw sewage into local waterways. This incident underscores the importance of risk identification and the dire consequences of inadequate system security.

4.2 Auditing Standards and Frameworks for SCADA/OT

Several standards and frameworks guide the auditing of SCADA and OT systems. Familiarity with these is crucial for any IT auditor.

- ISA/IEC 62443 : This international standard focuses on the security of industrial automation and control systems. It provides a systematic and practical approach to secure SCADA and OT systems.

- NIST SP 800-82 : Published by the National Institute of Standards and Technology, this guide focuses on Industrial Control System (ICS) security, offering recommendations and best practices.

- NERC CIP : The North American Electric Reliability Corporation's Critical Infrastructure Protection standards are designed for the electric utility industry, emphasizing the security and reliability of the electrical grid.

Example : The Stuxnet worm, discovered in 2010, specifically targeted SCADA systems used in nuclear facilities. By exploiting vulnerabilities in these systems, it caused significant physical damage. Adhering to the ISA/IEC 62443 standard could have potentially mitigated or even prevented this attack.

4.3 SCADA/OT Audit Process and Methodology

Auditing SCADA and OT systems is a systematic process that involves several steps:

1. Planning : Define the scope of the audit, identify key systems and components, and gather relevant documentation.

2.   Risk Assessment : Identify and rank potential vulnerabilities and threats based on their potential impact and likelihood of occurrence.

3.   Data Collection : Gather information through interviews, system reviews, and network scans.

4.   Analysis : Evaluate the collected data against the chosen standards and frameworks. Identify gaps, vulnerabilities, and areas of non-compliance.

5.   Reporting : Document findings, provide recommendations for improvement, and highlight areas of excellence.

6. Follow-up : Revisit the audited system after a specified period to assess the implementation of recommendations and ensure ongoing compliance.

Case Study: Ukraine Power Grid Attack (2015)

In December 2015, hackers launched a coordinated attack on Ukraine's power grid, causing blackouts across multiple regions. An audit prior to the attack could have identified vulnerabilities in their network, such as the use of outdated software and weak access controls. Proper remediation, guided by the audit findings, might have prevented or mitigated the attack.

In the world of SCADA and OT systems, the stakes are high. Effective auditing is not just a matter of compliance; it's a crucial tool to ensure the safety, security, and efficiency of critical infrastructure. As you navigate this realm, let this chapter serve as your foundation, guiding your approach and informing your decisions.

Chapter 5: Risk Assessment and
Management for SCADA/OT

Risk assessment and management are integral components of ensuring the security, reliability, and resilience of SCADA and OT systems. Given the critical nature of many operations relying on these systems – from power grids to water treatment facilities – understanding the risks and putting in place measures to manage them is paramount. This chapter delves deep into the process of identifying, assessing, and mitigating risks in SCADA and OT environments.

5.1 Identifying Risks in SCADA and OT Systems

Before any meaningful risk management can occur, one must first identify the potential risks. SCADA and OT systems, given their unique nature, have a distinct set of vulnerabilities.

- Hardware Risks : Physical damages, such as those due to natural disasters, sabotage, or wear and tear, can incapacitate critical components. For example, a flood in a power plant can damage control systems, leading to outages.

- Software Risks : Malware, software bugs, or incompatible updates can disrupt system operations. A real-world instance is the Stuxnet worm, which targeted SCADA systems and caused substantial damage.

- Communication Risks : SCADA and OT systems rely heavily on communication protocols. An interception or disruption in communication can compromise the system's integrity.

- Human Errors : Mistakes made during system configurations, maintenance, or operations can unintentionally introduce vulnerabilities.

- Supply Chain Risks : These arise from vulnerabilities in the supply chain, including compromised hardware or software components. The risks associated with third-party vendors and suppliers cannot be overlooked.

Exercise: List down all the hardware components, software applications, and communication protocols in your SCADA/OT environment. Beside each, note down potential risks, even if they seem minor.

5.2 Risk Assessment Methodologies

Once risks are identified, they need to be assessed in terms of their potential impact and likelihood. Several methodologies can be employed:

- Qualitative Risk Assessment : This method uses descriptive scales (e.g., low, medium, high) to evaluate the risks based on their potential severity and likelihood. It's more subjective but can be quicker to implement.

- Quantitative Risk Assessment : Quantitative methods involve numerical values, often monetary, to evaluate risks. It might involve calculating potential losses from a cyber breach or downtime due to equipment failure.

- Hybrid Methods : Combining both qualitative and quantitative approaches, hybrid methods aim to bring together the strengths of both methodologies.

A well-known framework for SCADA and OT risk assessment is the NIST SP 800-82, which provides guidance tailored for industrial control systems.

5.3 Risk Mitigation Strategies and Controls

Having identified and assessed the risks, the next step is to implement strategies and controls to manage them:

- Preventive Controls : These are designed to prevent a risk event from occurring. Examples include firewalls to prevent unauthorized access or training programs to reduce human error.

- Detective Controls : These controls detect and alert when a risk event occurs. Intrusion detection systems (IDS) in

SCADA networks or alarm systems in physical facilities are typical examples.

- Corrective Controls : Implemented post-event, these controls aim to restore systems to their normal state. Backup systems or disaster recovery plans are corrective controls.

- Compensating Controls : If a primary control isn't feasible, compensating controls provide an alternative means of risk mitigation. For instance, if a software patch for a known vulnerability isn't available, network segmentation might be used as a compensating control.

- Risk Transfer : Sometimes, it's more feasible to transfer the risk elsewhere, like purchasing insurance.

- Risk Avoidance : In scenarios where risks are too high, the best strategy might be to avoid them altogether. For instance, if a software update poses significant risks, delaying its deployment might be wise.

- Risk Acceptance : In cases where the cost of mitigation outweighs the potential impact, risks might be accepted knowingly.

Exercise: For each risk identified in your SCADA/OT environment, decide which mitigation strategy is most appropriate. Document the rationale behind each decision.

Conclusion

Risk assessment and management in SCADA and OT systems is an ongoing process. With the evolving nature of threats, regular reassessments and updates to mitigation strategies are essential. By understanding potential risks, assessing their impact, and implementing robust controls, you can ensure the security and resilience of your SCADA/OT environment.

Chapter 6: Auditing SCADA and OT Network Infrastructure

With the convergence of IT and OT, the network infrastructure supporting SCADA and OT systems has become a critical focal point for auditors. Ensuring the security, integrity, and resilience of this infrastructure is paramount. In this chapter, we will delve into the key aspects of SCADA and OT network infrastructure, exploring how to audit them effectively.

6.1 Network Segmentation and Isolation

Network segmentation refers to the division of a computer network into sub-networks, each being a network segment. In SCADA and OT systems, this is crucial for ensuring that an issue or breach in one segment doesn't compromise the entire system.

Key Concepts :
- VLANs (Virtual Local Area Networks) : These are used to group together devices

with similar security needs, irrespective of their physical location.

- DMZ (Demilitarized Zone) : A logical or physical subnet used to separate internal networks from external ones, like the internet.

Why is Segmentation Important?
- It limits the spread of malware and attacks.
- It reduces congestion and boosts performance.
- It enhances privacy and security by limiting access to sensitive information.

Auditing Network Segmentation:

1. Map the Network : Begin by creating a detailed map of the network. This should include all devices, their connections, and the various network segments.

Activity : Take a look at your current network diagram. Identify areas where segmentation can be improved.

2. Verify Isolation : Ensure that segments meant to be isolated from each other truly are. For example, the SCADA control network should be isolated from the business network.

Exercise : Attempt to communicate from one segment to another that should be isolated. If communication is possible, it's a red flag.

3. Check Access Controls : Verify that only authorized devices and users can access each segment. This often involves checking firewall rules and access control lists.

Case Study : The Stuxnet worm spread across segments in nuclear facilities, causing significant damage. Proper segmentation and isolation would have contained its spread.

Templates & Tools :

- Network Mapping Tools: Tools like Nmap and Wireshark can help auditors visualize the network.

- Access Control Checklist: A template detailing which users and devices should have access to each segment.

Audit Checklist :

1. Verify that sensitive OT systems are isolated from the broader IT network.
2. Ensure that access controls are implemented at each network boundary.
3. Confirm that VLAN configurations are secure and reviewed regularly.

6.2 Monitoring and Intrusion Detection

Monitoring is the continuous observation of a network to detect anomalies, while intrusion detection involves identifying unauthorized access or breaches.

Importance of Monitoring & Intrusion Detection :

- Quick identification of issues or breaches.

- Historical data for forensic analysis.

- Compliance with regulatory requirements.

Auditing Monitoring & Intrusion Detection :

1. Review Monitoring Policies : Understand what is being monitored, how often, and who reviews the logs.

Activity : Review a random sample of logs. Look for any anomalies and trace their resolution.

2. Assess Intrusion Detection Systems (IDS) : Ensure that the IDS is appropriately configured, updated, and actively monitoring all critical points in the network.

Exercise : Introduce a test threat (with prior permission) and observe if the IDS detects and alerts it.

3. Incident Response Integration : Ensure that there's a procedure to respond to the alerts generated by the IDS.

Case Study : A water facility in Florida was breached, but quick detection and response prevented any real-world harm.

Audit Checklist :

1. Ensure that all network traffic within the SCADA and OT environment is monitored.
2. Confirm that alerts are reviewed regularly and that there's a procedure for escalation.
3. Check for regular updates and patches to IDS and SIEM systems.

6.3 Secure Communication and Encryption

As SCADA and OT systems often communicate critical and sensitive data, ensuring the security of this communication is paramount.

Why Secure Communication?
- Protect data from eavesdropping.
- Ensure data integrity.
- Validate the authenticity of communication endpoints.

Auditing Secure Communication & Encryption :

1. Review Communication Protocols : Determine which protocols are in use and whether they are known to be secure. Protocols like SSL/TLS should be in use for secure communications.

Activity : List all communication protocols in use. Cross-reference with known vulnerabilities.

2. Check Encryption Implementation : Ensure that data at rest and in transit is encrypted using robust algorithms.

Exercise : Intercept a data packet (with permission) and attempt to decrypt it. If successful, it indicates weak encryption.

3. Validate Certificate Management : For systems using certificates for encryption, ensure they're valid, updated, and securely stored.

Case Study : The Heartbleed bug exploited vulnerabilities in the SSL/TLS encryption protocol, emphasizing the need for secure communication.

Templates & Tools :

- Encryption Checklist: A template detailing the encryption methods in use and their respective strengths.

- Communication Protocol Review Tool: Software that can identify and assess the communication protocols in use.

Audit Checklist :

1. Ensure that all data in transit, both internally and externally, is encrypted.

2. Confirm that VPNs are used for remote access and are secured with multi-factor authentication.

3. Regularly review and update encryption protocols and certificates.

Conclusion :

Auditing the network infrastructure of SCADA and OT systems is a vital step in ensuring the security and resilience of these systems. By understanding and implementing the guidelines and exercises in this chapter, auditors can be better equipped to assess and enhance the security posture of SCADA and OT environments.

Chapter 7: Auditing Physical Security and
Environment

In the world of SCADA and OT systems, while the focus often shifts to the intricacies of software and network security, the importance of physical security and environmental controls cannot be overstated. Physical breaches can lead to direct access to sensitive systems, potential tampering, and even catastrophic environmental damages. This chapter delves deep into the critical aspects of auditing physical security and environment for SCADA and OT systems.

7.1 Facility Access Control

Physical security starts with controlling who can enter a facility. Unauthorized access can lead to data breaches, equipment tampering, or even physical harm to the infrastructure.

Key Elements of Facility Access Control:

- Entry and Exit Points : Identify all possible entry and exit points in the facility, including main entrances, emergency exits, loading docks, and even seemingly insignificant access points like ventilation systems or utility rooms.

- Authentication Mechanisms : Examine the methods used to authenticate individuals before granting access. Common mechanisms include key cards, biometric scanners, pin codes, and physical keys.

- Visitor Management : Understand the protocols for allowing visitors into the facility. Are they logged? Are they always escorted?

Activities and Exercises :
1. Access Point Identification : On a blueprint of the facility, mark all potential entry and exit points. Consider how each can be a potential vulnerability.

2.   Role Play : Engage in a role-playing exercise where one team tries to gain unauthorized access, and another team tries to prevent it, highlighting potential weaknesses in the system.

Case Study: The Forgotten Backdoor :
In a renowned data center, while the main entrance had biometric authentication, a backdoor used by janitorial staff was overlooked and only had a basic lock. This oversight led to a significant breach when unauthorized individuals gained access through this door.

7.2 Environmental Controls

Environmental controls ensure that the facility maintains conditions optimal for equipment operation and data safety.

Key Elements of Environmental Controls :

- Temperature and Humidity : Ensure there are systems in place to maintain optimal temperature and humidity levels. Overheating can lead to equipment failure, and high humidity can cause condensation and corrosion.

- Fire Suppression : Examine the facility's fire suppression systems. Traditional sprinkler systems can damage equipment; thus, alternatives like gas-based suppression systems might be preferred.

- Flood Prevention : Especially important for facilities in flood-prone areas. Look for elevated equipment, flood barriers, and water detection systems.

Activities and Exercises :

1. Simulate a Power Outage : How do environmental controls respond in the event

of a power outage? Is there a backup power source, and how quickly does it activate?

2. Measure and Monitor : Use temperature and humidity loggers to measure conditions over a week. Are they consistent?

Case Study: The Costly Sprinkler Mistake :
A minor fire in a facility led to the activation of traditional sprinklers. While the fire was quickly contained, the water damage to the servers and equipment amounted to millions in losses.

7.3   Equipment   Protection   and Maintenance

Ensuring that the equipment is both protected from external threats and maintained regularly is crucial for the longevity and security of SCADA and OT systems.

Key Elements of Equipment Protection and Maintenance :

- Physical Barriers : Examine the barriers around critical equipment. Are they housed in cages or locked rooms?

- Maintenance Logs : Regular maintenance can identify potential issues before they become critical. Ensure there's a log of all maintenance activities and that they occur at regular intervals.

- Redundancy : For critical systems, is there a backup in place? If one piece of equipment fails, is there a replacement readily available?

Activities and Exercises :

1. Equipment Check : Randomly select a piece of equipment and trace its maintenance history. Was it serviced regularly? Were any issues noted and addressed?

2. Redundancy Test : Simulate the failure of a critical system. How quickly can operations be transferred to the backup?

Case Study: The Backup That Wasn't :
A critical server in an energy company failed. While there was a backup server in place, it hadn't been maintained or updated, leading to significant downtime and financial losses.

By understanding and implementing rigorous physical security and environmental controls, a facility can ensure the safety and efficiency of its SCADA and OT systems. Regular audits, as detailed in this chapter, will help identify potential vulnerabilities and rectify them before they can be exploited.

Chapter 8: Auditing Human Factors and Training

The technical components of SCADA and OT systems are undeniably crucial, but it's essential to remember that these systems are operated, maintained, and managed by people. Human factors, thus, play a pivotal role in the security and reliability of these systems. In this chapter, we'll delve into the importance of understanding and auditing the human elements of SCADA and OT systems, focusing on insider threats, training, and incident response preparedness.

8.1 Insider Threats and User Privileges

Definition and Importance : An insider threat arises when individuals within an organization misuse their authorized access to harm the organization either intentionally or unintentionally. Considering that SCADA and OT systems control critical infrastructure, the potential impact of insider threats is magnified.

Activity : Take a moment to think about a recent news story or case study involving an insider threat. What were the consequences? How could it have been prevented?

User Privileges : In SCADA and OT systems, user privileges define what actions a user can perform. Overly generous privileges can lead to unintentional mistakes or intentional misuse.

Exercise : Review the user privilege settings in a mock SCADA system. Identify any overly broad permissions and consider the potential risks associated with them.

Auditing for Insider Threats :
1. Access Review : Regularly review and audit user access rights. Ensure that

individuals only have access to the systems and data they need.

2.   Behavioral Monitoring : Use tools and software to monitor user behavior and identify any unusual or suspicious activities.

3. Whistleblower Policies : Ensure that there are clear and confidential channels for employees to report concerns about colleagues' behavior.

Case Study : In 2010, a disgruntled employee at a water treatment plant used his insider access to manipulate the system, leading to potential harm. This incident could have been prevented with stricter access controls and behavior monitoring.

8.2 Training and Awareness Programs

Why It Matters : A well-informed team is the first line of defense against potential threats. Training and awareness programs equip staff with the knowledge and skills they need to identify and respond to threats.

Activity : Think about a time when training helped you avoid a mistake at work. Share this experience with a colleague.

Key Components of Effective Training :

1. Relevance : Training should be tailored to the specific roles and responsibilities of the staff.

2. Frequency : Regular refresher courses ensure that staff stay updated with the latest threats and best practices.

3. Engagement : Use interactive methods like workshops, simulations, and hands-on exercises.

Exercise : Design a short training module on the importance of strong password practices for SCADA systems. Include interactive elements to engage learners.

Auditing Training Programs :

1. Content Review : Ensure that training materials are up-to-date and relevant.

2. Feedback Collection : Gather feedback from staff to identify areas for improvement.

3. Effectiveness Measurement : Use quizzes, simulations, and real-world scenarios to measure the effectiveness of training.

Case Study : A phishing attack targeted an energy company's SCADA system. Although the email looked genuine, a staff member who had recently undergone awareness training identified it as suspicious and reported it, preventing potential harm.

8.3 Incident Response Preparedness

The Need for Preparedness : Incidents are inevitable. What distinguishes organizations is how they respond. A well-prepared team can minimize damage, recover faster, and learn from incidents.

Activity : Recall a recent incident, either from the news or personal experience. How was the response? What could have been done differently?

Key Elements of Incident Response :
1. Identification : Recognizing the signs of an incident promptly.
2. Containment : Limiting the damage and preventing further harm.
3. Eradication : Finding and eliminating the root cause.
4. Recovery : Restoring systems to normal operations.

5. Lessons Learned : Analyzing the incident to prevent future occurrences.

Exercise : Conduct a tabletop exercise simulating a cyberattack on a SCADA system. Discuss the steps you would take in response.

Auditing Incident Response Preparedness :
1. Plan Review : Ensure that the incident response plan is comprehensive and up-to-date.
2. Drill Evaluation : Observe incident response drills and identify areas for improvement.
3. Post-Incident Analysis : Review the response to past incidents to identify lessons learned.

Case Study : In 2015, an energy company experienced a ransomware attack. Thanks to their robust incident response plan, they were able to contain the attack quickly, minimizing downtime and financial impact.

Conclusion

Human factors play a crucial role in the security and reliability of SCADA and OT systems. By understanding and addressing insider threats, investing in training and awareness, and preparing for incidents, organizations can significantly enhance their resilience.

Chapter 9: Auditing Backup and Recovery Procedures

In the realm of SCADA and OT systems, the importance of backups and disaster recovery cannot be overstated. These systems, responsible for critical operations, need robust backup procedures and disaster recovery plans to ensure continuity and resilience against unforeseen events. This chapter provides an in-depth exploration of auditing these vital processes.

9.1 Backup Strategies and Schedules for SCADA and OT Systems

Understanding Backup Strategies : Backups for SCADA and OT systems aren't just about duplicating data. It's about ensuring that operational continuity is maintained even in the face of catastrophic system failures.

- Full Backups : This strategy involves taking a backup of the entire system. While thorough, it requires significant storage space and time.

- Incremental Backups : Here, only the changes made since the last backup are stored. It's faster and requires less storage but necessitates a full backup at regular intervals.

- Differential Backups : This method saves the changes made since the last full backup, offering a middle ground between full and incremental backups.

Scheduling Backups : Timing is crucial. For systems that are constantly operational, backups should be scheduled during off-peak hours to minimize disruptions. Regular testing of backups is also vital to ensure they are functional.

Exercise : Analyze the backup strategy of a hypothetical SCADA system. What are its strengths and weaknesses? How would you optimize its backup schedule?

9.2 Data Integrity and Validation for SCADA and OT Systems

Ensuring Data Integrity : A backup is only as good as its integrity. SCADA and OT systems should employ checksums and hash algorithms to ensure data remains uncorrupted during backup processes.

- Checksums : A simple method where the sum of all bytes in a file is computed and stored. During restoration, if the checksum doesn't match, the data might be corrupted.

- Hash Algorithms : More complex than checksums, they produce a unique fixed-size string of bytes from data. Any slight change in data results in a drastically different hash.

Validation Tools : Post-backup validation is essential. Tools that can simulate data restoration without actually overwriting current data are invaluable in ensuring backup reliability.

Exercise : Using a set of sample data, compute its checksum and hash. Modify a tiny portion of this data and recompute. Observe the changes.

Challenges :
1. Real-time data changes in OT systems can lead to inconsistencies during backup.
2. Vulnerabilities in backup software can lead to data corruption.

3. Physical damages like disk failures can compromise data integrity.

Steps for Validation :

1. Use data validation tools after every backup.

2. Perform random spot checks to ensure data consistency.

3. Maintain logs of all backup activities for audit purposes.

4. Regularly update and patch backup software to mitigate vulnerabilities.

Best Practices :

- Schedule full backups during off-peak hours.

- Utilize differential or incremental backups for frequent, smaller backups.

- Regularly test and validate backups to ensure they're functional and relevant.

9.3 Disaster Recovery Planning for SCADA and OT Systems

Importance of a Disaster Recovery Plan (DRP) : A DRP isn't just about restoring data. It's a comprehensive plan detailing how operations will be resumed after a disaster.

Key Components of a DRP :
1.   Risk Assessment : Identify potential threats and their impacts.
2.   Resource Allocation : Determine what resources (human, technical, financial) will be needed in the event of a disaster.
3.   Communication Plan : Establish clear channels of communication for all stakeholders during a disaster.
4. Mock Recovery Drills : Regularly simulate disaster scenarios to test the effectiveness of the DRP.

Case Study : In 2019, a major energy company faced a ransomware attack. Their DRP, which had been regularly tested and updated, allowed them to restore operations within hours, minimizing financial and operational impacts.

Exercise : Draft a basic DRP for a mock SCADA system. Consider potential threats like natural disasters, cyber-attacks, and equipment failures.

Steps to Test and Validate :
1. Conduct regular disaster recovery drills.
2. Document findings and areas of improvement.
3. Update the plan based on drill outcomes.

Conclusion

Backup and disaster recovery are pillars of resilience for SCADA and OT systems. Proper strategies, combined with regular audits, can ensure that these systems remain operational even in the face of adversity.

Chapter10: Compliance and Regulatory Considerations

As SCADA (Supervisory Control and Data Acquisition) and OT (Operational Technology) systems play increasingly critical roles in modern infrastructure and industry, ensuring that these systems adhere to global regulations becomes paramount. The world of compliance and regulation is vast, and for auditors, understanding this landscape is essential not only for the sake of legality but also to ensure the safety, reliability, and resilience of the systems they oversee.

Overview of Relevant Regulations

In the realm of SCADA and OT, regulations are not just bureaucratic hurdles; they are safety nets, designed to ensure that these vital systems operate securely and efficiently.

Why Regulations are Crucial : At their core, SCADA and OT systems control and monitor real-world processes, from power generation to water treatment. A failure in these systems can lead to real-world consequences, including service disruptions, financial losses, environmental damage, or even loss of life. Regulations help set a standard of operation, ensuring that these systems are both safe and effective.

Key Global Regulations Impacting SCADA and OT :

1. NERC CIP (North America) : Originating in the aftermath of a significant blackout in 2003, the North American Electric Reliability Corporation's Critical Infrastructure Protection (NERC CIP) standards focus on the bulk power system's reliability. They outline cybersecurity requirements for entities under their jurisdiction.

2. EU NIS Directive (Europe) : The European Union's Directive on Security of Network and

Information Systems (NIS Directive) is the first piece of EU-wide legislation on cybersecurity. It provides legal measures to ensure a high common level of network and information security across the Union.

3. ISA/IEC 62443 (International) : A series of standards focusing on industrial automation and control systems security, these outline best practices and are widely regarded as the gold standard in the industry.

Regulatory Bodies : These regulations are overseen by a mixture of governmental and non-governmental organizations, depending on the region. Familiarity with the local regulatory body is crucial for any auditor, as these entities often provide guidance, updates, and resources related to the regulations they oversee.

Ensuring Compliance during Audits

Audits are more than just checks; they are opportunities to align SCADA and OT systems with global best practices and regulations.

Significance of Compliance : Non-compliance can result in penalties, operational disruptions, and reputational damage. More importantly, non-compliance can indicate vulnerabilities in the system, leaving it open to potential threats.

Strategies for Ensuring Compliance :

1. Continuous Monitoring : Rather than treating audits as periodic events, organizations should engage in continuous monitoring of their systems, ensuring they always remain compliant.

2. Use of Compliance Tools : Numerous software solutions can help automate the compliance process, checking system configurations, access controls, and other parameters against regulatory standards.

3. Training and Awareness : Ensuring that all stakeholders, from operators to top management, understand the importance of compliance and their role in ensuring it.

Case Study : In 2019, a major utility company faced hefty fines due to non-compliance with NERC CIP standards. An audit revealed lapses in access controls and system monitoring. In the aftermath, the company invested heavily in training and compliance tools, transforming their approach to SCADA and OT system management.

Legal and Ethical Considerations in Auditing

Beyond the technical and procedural aspects of auditing lies the domain of ethics and legality.

Legal Ramifications : Non-compliance can lead to legal penalties, often proportional to the potential harm that could result from a system failure. Auditors must be aware of these potential penalties as they can guide the urgency and focus of their audits.

Ethical Obligations : Auditors must operate with integrity, objectivity, and professionalism. Their primary duty is to the truth, ensuring that SCADA and OT systems are safe, secure, and efficient.

Navigating Ethical Dilemmas : There may be times when auditors face pressure to overlook certain findings or to prioritize certain audits over others. In these situations, auditors must fall back on their professional standards, seeking guidance from peers or industry bodies if needed.

Example : An auditor discovers a minor non-compliance issue but is pressured by the organization to overlook it due to the potential costs of remediation. Instead of acquiescing, the auditor documents the issue, communicates its potential implications, and works with the organization to find a cost-effective solution.

In conclusion, compliance and regulatory considerations are not just boxes to be ticked; they are essential components of the auditing process, ensuring that SCADA and OT systems operate safely, securely, and effectively. As the regulatory landscape evolves, auditors must stay informed, ensuring that they continue to provide value to the organizations they serve.

Chapter11: Reporting and Follow-Up of Audit Findings on SCADA and OT Systems

Effective auditing of SCADA and OT systems is not just about identifying vulnerabilities and weaknesses. It is also about ensuring that these findings are communicated effectively and acted upon promptly. In this chapter, we will explore the stages of post-audit activities, focusing on reporting, communication, and follow-up actions.

Structuring the Audit Report for SCADA and OT Systems

An audit report is a formal record of the findings and recommendations from an audit. For SCADA and OT systems, this report should be both detailed and clear.

Essential Elements :
1. Executive Summary : A brief overview of the audit's scope, objectives, methodology, major findings, and key recommendations.

2. Detailed Findings : A comprehensive breakdown of all vulnerabilities, weaknesses, and issues identified during the audit.

3. Recommendations : Specific, actionable steps that the organization should take to address each finding.

4. Supporting Evidence : Screenshots, logs, and other evidence that supports each finding.

5. Appendices : Additional information, such as detailed technical data, a glossary of terms, and references.

Importance of Clarity and Precision : The audit report will be read by a variety of stakeholders, from technical experts to top management. It's crucial that the report is written in clear, precise language, free of jargon, and easily understood by all readers.

Organizing Information : Group findings by severity or system component. Use headings, subheadings, bullet points, and numbered lists for easy navigation. Incorporate charts and graphs to visually represent data.

Example : In a real-world audit of a power plant's SCADA system, the audit report highlighted a critical vulnerability in the system's communication protocol. The report included clear evidence, a detailed description of the potential impact, and specific remediation steps, leading to prompt action by the plant's management.

Communicating Findings and Recommendations for SCADA and OT Systems

Once the audit report is ready, the next step is effective communication.

Best Practices :

1.   Tailored Presentations : Different stakeholders will have different needs. Technical teams will want detailed insights, while executive leadership will be more interested in high-level findings and business impact. Tailor your presentations accordingly.

2.   Use Visual Aids : Charts, graphs, and infographics can simplify complex data and make your findings more impactful.

3.   Feedback Sessions : Allow stakeholders to ask questions and seek clarifications during your presentations.

4.   Written Communication : In addition to presentations, provide written summaries or briefs for stakeholders to review at their convenience.

Example : At a manufacturing company, the audit team used a combination of detailed reports, visual presentations, and interactive workshops to communicate their findings. This multi-pronged approach ensured that all stakeholders, from the factory floor to the boardroom, understood the audit's implications.

Audit Follow-up and Remediation for SCADA and OT Systems

The audit process doesn't end with the report. Ensuring that the recommendations are implemented is critical.

Post-Audit Activities :

1. Track Implementation : Use a tracking system or software to monitor the progress of each recommendation's implementation.
2. Verification : Once a recommendation has been implemented, verify its effectiveness. This could involve re-testing, reviewing documentation, or other methods.

3. Feedback Loops : Maintain open channels of communication with the organization. Gather feedback on the audit process, findings, and recommendations to refine future audits.

Challenges : Organizations may lack the resources or expertise to implement recommendations. In such cases, auditors should be prepared to provide additional guidance or suggest alternative solutions.

Example : An audit of a city's water treatment plant identified several vulnerabilities in its OT system. The audit team maintained a close relationship with the plant's management, providing additional training and resources to ensure effective remediation. Six months later, a follow-up audit showed significant improvements.

Tips for Auditors :

1. Always seek feedback and be open to refining your approach.

2. Stay updated with the latest developments in SCADA and OT systems to provide the most relevant recommendations.

3. Build strong relationships with stakeholders to ensure effective communication and follow-up.

Conclusion

Auditing SCADA and OT systems is a meticulous process that extends beyond the identification of vulnerabilities. Properly structured reports, effective communication, and diligent follow-up ensure that the audit's findings lead to tangible improvements in system security and resilience.

Appendix

- Access Control : Mechanisms that determine who can access a system and what operations they can perform once they have access.

- Audit : A systematic review and examination of systems and operations to ensure compliance with established criteria.

- Behavioral Monitoring : The process of tracking, logging, and analyzing the actions of users within a system.

- Compliance : Adherence to regulations, standards, or specified requirements.

- Cybersecurity : The practice of protecting systems, networks, and programs from digital attacks.

- Data Historian : A centralized database used in OT and SCADA systems to record high-frequency operational data over time.

- HMI (Human-Machine Interface) : The user interface that connects operators to the controller in SCADA and OT systems.

- Incident Response : The organized approach addressing and managing the aftermath of a security breach or cyberattack.

- Insider Threat : A security threat that originates from within the organization, such as employees, former employees, or contractors.

- IT (Information Technology) : The use of systems, especially computers and telecommunications, to store, retrieve, and transmit information.

- Network Segmentation : The practice of dividing a computer network into sub-networks to improve performance and security.

- OT (Operational Technology) : Hardware and software that detects or causes changes in physical processes through direct monitoring and/or control of physical devices.

- PLC (Programmable Logic Controller) : A digital computer used for automation of electromechanical processes.

- Privilege : A user's rights or permissions in a system that determine what actions they can perform.

- RTU (Remote Terminal Unit) : A device installed in remote locations that collect data, and then send it back to a central location (such as a SCADA system).

- SCADA (Supervisory Control and Data Acquisition) : A control system architecture comprising computers, networked data communications, and graphical user interfaces for high-level supervision of processes.

- Threat Landscape : The collection of threats that an organization might face at any given time.

- User Privileges : The rights or permissions granted to users in the context of IT and OT systems.

- Whistleblower : An individual who exposes information or activity deemed illegal, unethical, or not correct within an organization.

References and Further Readings

- Smith, S. (2018). An Introduction to SCADA and OT Systems. Tech Publishers.
- Johnson, M. (2015). Evolution of SCADA: Past, Present, and Future. Industrial Journal.
- Davis, L. (2020). The Role of SCADA in Modern Industrial Operations. Automation Today
- Thompson, R. (2019). IT vs. OT: Bridging the Gap. TechWorld Journal.
- Smith, J. (2015). Introduction to PLCs: A beginner's guide. Automation World.

- Johnson, R. (2018). IEDs in modern power systems. PowerGrid International.
- Mitchell, B. (2020). Human-Machine Interfaces in Industrial Systems. TechTarget.
- Anderson, M. (2019). SCADA Systems and Their Role in Modern Infrastructure. Control Engineering Daily.
- Tanenbaum, A. S., & Wetherall, D. J. (2011). Computer networks. Prentice Hall.
- Clarke, S. (2017). Communication protocols in SCADA. Industrial Automation Journal.
- Palmer, D. (2021). The rise of remote access in SCADA systems. Cyber Security Magazine.
- Zetter, K. (2014). "Countdown to Zero Day: Stuxnet and the Launch of the World's First Digital Weapon". Crown.

- Lee, R. M., Assante, M. J., & Conway, T. (2016). "Analysis of the Cyber Attack on the Ukrainian Power Grid". SANS Industrial Control Systems.
- "TRITON: The First ICS Cyber Attack on Safety Instrument Systems". FireEye. (2017).
- Industrial Communication Networks - Network and System Security*, by R. Zurawski, 2014
- Security for Critical Infrastructure SCADA Systems*, S. Oman, and E. Schweitzer, 2003
- NIST Special Publication 800-82: *Guide to Industrial Control Systems (ICS) Security*
- ISA/IEC 62443 series of standards
- Hurricane Katrina Impact Report (https://www.usgs.gov/centers/wgsc/science/hurricane-katrina-impact-studies?qt-

science_center_objects=0#qt-science_center_objects)

- Symantec's Deep Dive on Stuxnet (https://www.symantec.com/content/en/us/enterprise/media/security_response/whitepapers/w32_stuxnet_dossier.pdf)
- Maroochy Shire Sewage Spill (https://www.csoonline.com/article/2117849/maroochy-shire-sewage-spill.html)
- [NIST SP 800-82: Guide to Industrial Control Systems (ICS) Security (https://csrc.nist.gov/publications/detail/sp/800-82/rev-2/final)
- Zetter, K. (2014). An Unprecedented Look at Stuxnet, the World's First Digital Weapon.

- Stamatis, D. H. (2003). *Failure Mode and Effect Analysis: FMEA from

Theory to Execution*. ASQ Quality Press.

- Lee, R. M., Assante, M. J., & Conway, T. (2016). Analysis of the Cyber Attack on the Ukrainian Power Grid. SANS Industrial Control Systems.

- Intrusion Detection in SCADA Systems (https://www.researchgate.net/publication/)

- Physical Security and Environmental Protection , John O. Harris, CRC Press, 2012.

- Effective Physical Security , Lawrence Fennelly, Butterworth-Heinemann, 2016.

- Smith, R. (2019). Physical Security in the Digital Age. CyberTech Publications.

- O'Donnell, L. (2020). Environmental Controls for Data Centers. IT Pro Press.

- Insider Threats in Critical Infrastructure: A Brief Overview. (2018). International Journal of Critical Infrastructure Protection .
- Training for Cybersecurity: Current Trends and Future Needs. (2020). Cybersecurity Training Journal .
- Best Practices for Incident Response in SCADA Systems. (2017). SCADA Security Review .
- "Insider Threats in SCADA Systems" - SCADA Security Journal, 2020.
- "Effective Training Techniques for OT Professionals" - OT Training Quarterly, 2019.
- "Incident Response in Modern OT Environments" - Industrial Cybersecurity Review, 2021.
- Smith, A. (2017). Backup Strategies for Industrial Control Systems . TechInsights Journal.

- Johnson, K. & Lee, M. (2018). Data Integrity in OT Systems: Challenges and Solutions . OT Security Review.
- Davis, R. (2019). Disaster Recovery Planning for SCADA Systems . SCADA Resilience Reports.
- NIST Special Publication 800-82 : This guide provides an overview of security for industrial control systems, including SCADA systems. It includes recommendations and templates for risk assessment, system characterization, and threat identification.
- [NIST SP 800-82](https://csrc.nist.gov/publications/detail/sp/800-82/rev-2/final)
- ISACA : The Information Systems Audit and Control Association (ISACA) offers various resources, including templates and tools for IT auditors,

some of which are applicable to SCADA and OT systems.

- [ISACA Audit Tools and Techniques](https://www.isaca.org/resources/tools-and-techniques)
- SANS Institute : The SANS Institute provides resources on Industrial Control Systems (ICS) security, including checklists and templates for SCADA and OT systems.
- [SANS ICS Resources](https://www.sans.org/industrial-control-systems-security)
- ISA/IEC 62443 Standards : These standards focus on the security of industrial automation and control systems. While they're primarily standards, they offer a structured approach that can be transformed into audit templates.
- [ISA/IEC 62443 Overview](https://www.isa.org/standar

ds-and-publications/isa-
standards/standards-view/isa-62443-
series-standards)
- Center for Internet Security (CIS)
  Controls : CIS provides best practice
  guidelines, and while they're not
  SCADA-specific, they're adaptable for
  SCADA environments. The CIS
  Controls Self-Assessment Tool can be
  particularly useful.
- [CIS
  Controls](https://www.cisecurity.org/c
  ontrols/)
- PAS Global : They offer solutions for
  ICS cybersecurity, safety, and
  compliance. Their resources section
  might have templates and white
  papers useful for SCADA/OT Systems
  Auditors.
  (https://www.pas.com/resources)
- SCADAhacker : This website offers a
  range of resources, including tools,

templates, and best practices specifically focused on SCADA and ICS systems. (https://www.scadahacker.com/library.html)

- Templates.net : This platform offers a variety of generic audit report templates that can be adapted for SCADA/OT systems. (https://www.templates.net/editable/audit)

- GitHub : Many professionals and organizations share their audit templates and tools on GitHub. A search for "SCADA audit templates" or "OT system audit templates" might yield relevant results. (https://github.com/)

- Vendor-Specific Resources : Often, vendors of SCADA/OT systems provide their own best practices, guidelines, and templates. It's a good practice to check with specific SCADA/OT system vendors for their proprietary resources.

- ICS-CERT (Industrial Control Systems Cyber Emergency Response Team): Offers a range of resources, advisories, and alerts for industrial control systems. (https://us-cert.cisa.gov/ics)
- SANS Institute : Provides training, research, and certifications related to ICS and SCADA security. (https://www.sans.org/industrial-control-systems-security/)
- ISA99/IEC 62443 : Standards and guidelines focused on the security of industrial automation and control systems. (https://www.isa.org/standards-and-publications/isa-standards/isa-standards-committees/isa99/)

-   NIST Special Publication 800-82 :
    Guide to Industrial Control Systems
    (ICS) Security.

    (https://csrc.nist.gov/publications/detai
    l/sp/800-82/final)
-   Journal of Cybersecurity & Privacy : An
    academic journal covering various
    cybersecurity topics, including ICS and
    SCADA systems.
    (https://journals.ub.uni-giessen.de/jcp)
-   Stouffer, K. A., Pillitteri, V. Y.,
    Lightman, S., Abrams, M., & Hahn, A.
    (2015). Guide to Industrial Control
    Systems (ICS) security . National
    Institute of Standards and Technology
    (NIST), Special Publication 800-82.
-   Langner, R. (2011). Stuxnet:
    Dissecting a cyberwarfare weapon .
    IEEE Security & Privacy, 9(3), 49-51.

- Beresford, D. (2011). Exploiting Siemens Simatic S7 PLCs . Black Hat USA.

- Butts, J., & Lowe, J. (2007). A framework for security analysis of SCADA control systems communications . In IEEE Power Engineering Society General Meeting, 1-8.

- Mitchell, R., & Chen, I. R. (2014). A survey of intrusion detection techniques for cyber-physical systems . ACM Computing Surveys (CSUR), 46(4), 1-29.

- Mansfield, L., & Ragsdale, D. (2008). Security challenges of small-scale SCADA systems . Journal of Computer Security, 16(5), 533-551.

- CRITIS : The International Conference on Critical (Information) Infrastructures Security. A platform for researchers and professionals from various disciplines to discuss the latest methods and technologies in the field. (https://www.critis2021.org/)

- ICS Cybersecurity Conference : One of the longest-running events dedicated to ICS cybersecurity, which brings together professionals and academics in the field. (https://www.icscybersecurityconference.com/)

- SCADAhacker : A resource offering a variety of materials, tools, and insights related to SCADA and ICS security. (https://www.scadahacker.com/)

- CyberX : Provides reports and whitepapers on various topics related to ICS and OT cybersecurity. (https://cyberx-labs.com/resources/)

www.ingramcontent.com/pod-product-compliance
Lightning Source LLC
Chambersburg PA
CBHW070853260726
48661CB00004B/1377